Top E-mail Marketing Tactics

HOT TIPS FOR ANY LIST

by
Lazaros Georgoulas

Independent researcher,
marketer and author:
http://amazon.com/author/lazarosgeorgoulas

E-mail me: lazageo@gmail.com

ISBN-13: 978-1499230338

ISBN-10: 1499230338

Disclaimer: The author has put all his efforts to present valid, accurate and fresh information to the user. But due to the changing nature of the internet, the author cannot be held responsible for the success or failure the reader will achieve after applying the tactics. You own your results and you must handle them.

Printed by CreateSpace, An Amazon.com company

"…I gathered the top 20+ e-mail marketing tips available online and I after hard split testing, I am revealing them here…"
Laz. A. Georgoulas – Nextnet Internet Services CEO

TABLE OF CONTENTS

First page

My quote

Introduction

#1: More than 1 link

#2: Use the Power of "PS"s

#3: Use e-mail variables wisely

#4: Use odd subject lines

#5: Utilize the "Thank You" page

#6: Offer a bonus if they click the link

#7: Create conflicts… create interest…

#8: Find the right subject lines

#9: Use a different "From:" e-mail address

#10: The "Do nothing e-mail"

#11: The magical URL

#12: The name of your URL/offer

#13: Your affiliate URL/username

#14: Improve your CALL TO ACTION

#15: Use Exit Pop-ups

#16: The magical archive

#17: Increase social activity with bonuses

#18: Ask people to add you to their contacts

#19: Use scarcity to increase open rate and click-through rate

#20: Resend the message to those who didn't open

#21: Use curiosity to increase clicks

#22: Take advantage of your Unsubscribes

#23: Blog your e-mail messages

Closing

Credits

Promotion

INTRODUCTION

Hello and thank for ordering this brief but powerful guid. It contains fresh stuff that really works (2014, 2015 and beyond) and if you have a mailing list or if you send e-mails to people expecting them to ACT on your messages, THEN you definitely need to know the tactics on this guide.

I want to believe that the information I am about to present you is different than anything you've read about. I want you to view e-mail marketing from a different angle. At least this was my goal. You, as a reader, will judge if my goal is complete.

I don't want to waste any more of your time so let's begin with the e-mail marketing tips!

But before that...

I want to make a personal disclaimer. The tips I present in this book is the result of several split tests me and my team have applied to our mailing lists.

Also, many tips (the really really good ones) are the result of conversation with top marketers and e-mail marketing industry experts.

The tips are here to give you new ideas, provide insight. The possibilities are endless. You understand that you must make your own tests to find out what works best for your industry/niche and the type of your list.

Most of the tips though are so…. "bound" to produce great results, the which I also hope for you!

THE GOAL OF ALL THIS IS TO MAKE MORE $$$ FROM YOUR E-MAIL MARKETING EFFORTS.-

NOW ON WITH THE E-MAIL MARKETING TACTICS… … …

TACTIC #1:

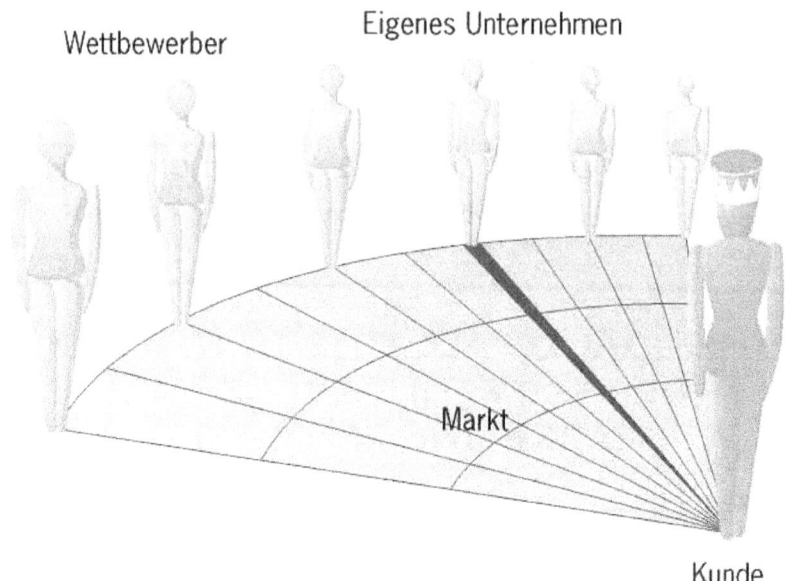

Wettbewerber | Eigenes Unternehmen | Markt | Kunde

This is somewhat common sense but I want to start lightly...

So the idea is to add more than one link in your e-mails.

It doesn't matter if it is the same link (actually this works even better) as long as it is "spread" evenly in the body of the e-mail.

Add a link at the beginning and a link at the bottom of the message. Maybe 2 more links in the body of the e-mail message body. More links, more clicks.-

I am subscribed to dozens of newsletters, mailing lists, update lists etc. I receive lots of e-mails with offers and these marketers only add a single link for the reader to click on.

No, I will not fall on that category...! I want more links and more click-juice... sometimes (joke)!

TACTIC #2:

Use the Power of "PSs"

This tactic is about always adding a "PS" at the end of your e-mail message followed by your link e.g.

"*PS: Blah blah blah blah click for more: http://mylovelysite.com*"

If you think about it, the "PS" is the last think the user sees and many people (like me) are going through their e-mails quickly because they receive lots of them.

So, if you allow users the chance to see a link at the end of your message, you increase the possibilities of him/her clicking the link.

TACTIC #3:

Use e-mail variables wisely

When I say variables I mean the subscriber's name or e-mail address. If you use online autoresponder services like GetResponse or AWeber it is easy to add these to your e-mails. So, people will see their name or personal e-mail address in your messages. OK, this is nice, personal and pretty common sense but guess what?

People are now familiar with all this subscribing processes and they are not impressed when they see their name in the greeting :/

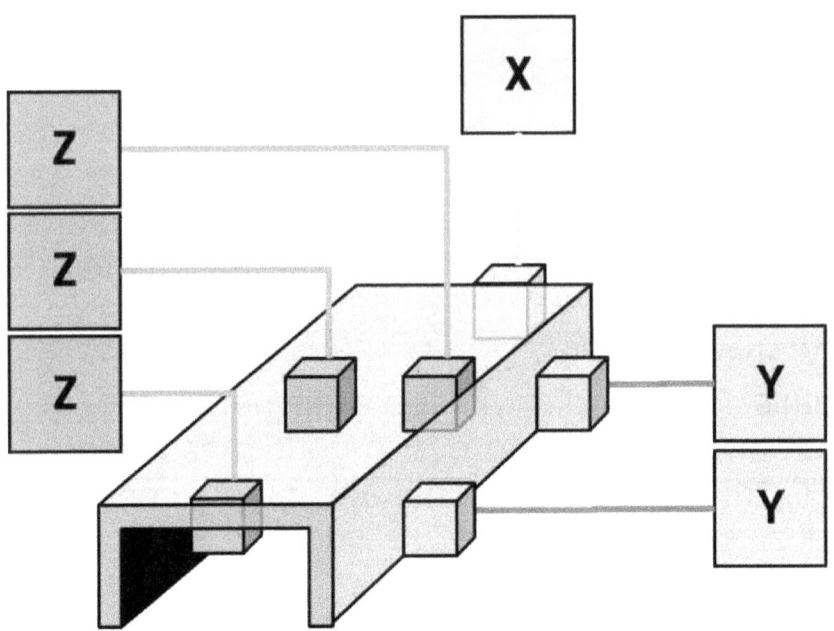

So, what you can do is something different that the user does not expect (of you course you should always test):

Instead of this...:
Hi {SubscriberName},
e.g. Hi Lazaros,

Try this (especially if you don't see many clicks)...:
Hi {SubscriberEmail},
e.g. Hi my@email.com,

or you can try this as a greeting:

Hello user,
Hello dear subscriber,
Hello valued customer/client,

Do not mention the variable at the beginning of the message. Instead you could use it surprisingly somewhere inside the e-mail body.

e.g.

"...and you know something {SubscriberName}?"
"...and you know something John?"

TACTIC #4:

This one is especially useful if you only get a few clicks or a low open-rate. The idea is to find a weird but solid subject line. This could include a quote from a conversation or words of wisdom from some ancient healer/prophet like Jesus Christ or Buddha etc.

Also, be sure to listen to what children say to other children or their parents. Youngsters produce excellent subject lines that catch attention.

But here's the catch. You have to make it sound like a real e-mail conversation, like you are replying to the subscriber, not like something you made up just to draw attention to another one of your offers.

The goal is of course, to make the user open the e-mail.

Here are some 'subject' examples:

1. *"I saw your site appearing on Yahoo OMG!"*
2. *"Then we both love that house"*
3. *"Hey, are you up late?"*

4. "Wow! is this your ad?"
5. "I saw your e-book"

Try to match the subject with your niche. Example #2 above refers to a house so this might be a good subject line for a semi-responsive mailing list with people interested in Real Estate matters.

I hope you get my idea... (I am sure you did.-)
Try it, test it especially if you are seeing low openings or low click-through rate.

TACTIC #5:

Utilize the "Thank You" page

When users add their e-mail (and name possibly) in your opt-in form to get in your list, you send them to a "Thank You" page. For most marketers this is a page that is not utilized at all...

For example, you can add a banner in that page directing to another one of your offers.

You can add an one time offer with a timer and run it legitimately every now and then.

You can also surprise the user with a freebie (e.g. a mini PDF report which will work as a sales funnel for another main offer/product of yours)

Another way to utilize the "Thank You" page is to add an affiliate offer/link/banner if you are signed up with networks like Clickbank or CommissionJunction.

There are tons of them but I believe the most profitable and solid for affiliate marketers is Clickbank.

Can you see the potential of this? The "Thank You" page is usually a static page where the user has no other choice but close the window. Well... utilize this page. Place ads, affiliate offers, banners, whatever to get the most from your subscriber (remember they are "hot" when they sign up)...

TACTIC #6:

Offer a bonus if they click the link

This is another very important strategy that has worked for me and I know it might work for most people who will read this book. That's because people like freebies and free things in general. This will never change.

So, the idea is to offer some type of bonus if the user clicks your links.

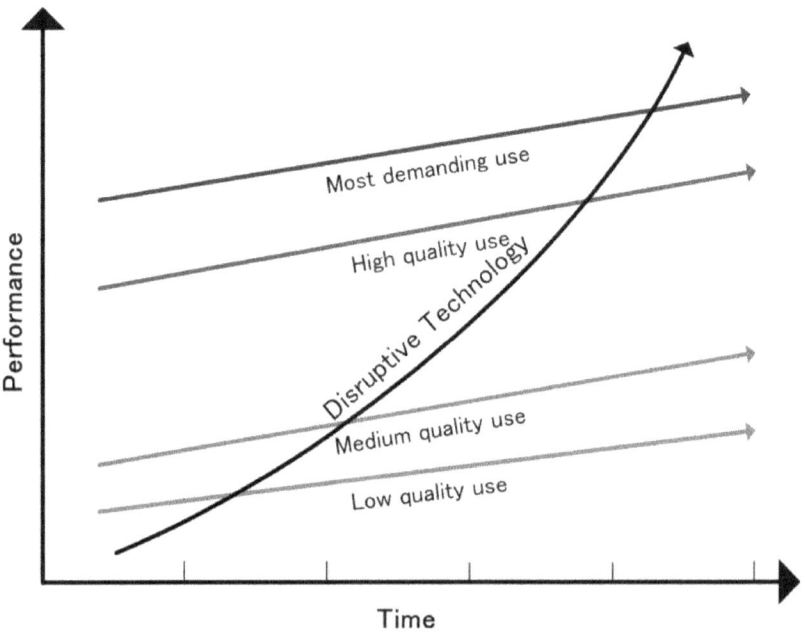

For example if you sell your own product, find some type of incentive that's related to the product and possibly enhancing it. Then in your e-mail message tell the people that if they click the link below and do what you want them to do, you will give them this very special and super related bonus.

That's one of the best strategies to incentivize clicks and get more of them of course. You can make the bonus a sales funnel for another product or service, an upgrade or it could be a high-paying and high-converting affiliate offer.

TACTIC #7:

Here we have something that's sometimes dangerous to apply, but if you don't get many clicks then it will not get worse. Instead, I believe it will attract attention and more of your subscribers will also want to e-mail you with comments and feedback.

So, you might also notice an increase in the number of e-mail replies you receive from your subscribers.

This strategy refers to the e-mail body where you try to tempt the user to click on your offer.

The whole idea is to create conflict around a topic related to your niche. For example if you own a football website and you sell football equipment you could create a conflict about the top 2 football teams of the league and pretend that you are a fan (or you support) team A while you express your "hatred" about team B, then you will create a conflict and a "buzz" among your e-mail subscribers.

A lot of them will be triggered and they will send you e-mails with either good or bad comments/words etc. But this will keep the minds of people around you and your subject and this will help promote your offers or products better.

I do not recommend using this tactic all the time. Select the best incident (timing matters) and take advantage of it to draw the attention of your subscribers to you and therefore to your products.

TACTIC #8:

Find the right subject lines

Not every audience is the same and there's no golden rule for the perfect subject line.

So, what you have to do is find the right TYPE of subject lines that make your subscribers open your e-mails and also prepare them to be 'ready and set' to click the links inside the body of your e-mails.

But, how to find the ideal subject line?

First of all, this is something that might change from time to time or as seasons pass. So, you have to split test.

One method that's been tried is to you select 4-6 completely different subject lines in terms of phrasing, length and formatting.

Make sure the subject line is strong and that it associates with the message in the body of your e-mail (90% of marketers do this wrong...!)

Then measure open rate and click through rate of your e-mails (you understand you MUST have a way to access such statistics). Locate which subject line produced the more clicks. This is the one you should try to use to bring more clicks and visitors to your offers.

A lot of list owners are simply happy just with a high "Open Rate". I believe this is wrong because a high open rate with a low click rate will not produce money/sales/visitors etc. What I am after is $$$. How about you?

TACTIC #9:

Use a different "From:" e-mail address

This one belongs to the "hacking" tactics that can produce amazing results. Don't worry it will not harm your subscribers or anyone else!

The idea is to use a different, more appealing e-mail address to the "From:" field. If you don't know how to do this with your mailing list software or autoresponder (highly unlikely) then consider changing mailing list software or autoresponder provider (joke!)...

If this is the case, simply discard this tip!

But anyway, I am pretty sure many people who read this, will be able to "manipulate" the "From:" field in their e-mail messages so it looks different than the original e-mail address. I mean...

...change it from:

john@mydomain.com

...to something like:

Johnny@mydomain.com

But why would you want to do that...?

Because the majority of your subscribers have white-listed the e-mail address you send your newsletter/mailings from. And they also use certain filters so as e-mails from a certain address go automatically to a certain folder. As a result your e-mails might end up in a folder for later use (who doesn't do that?). But who really goes through all the e-mails they store for later reading? Just a small percentage checks all these e-mails! So, if you change the "From:" field you will by-pass all these filters and you will also surprise the user ;) hopefully they will open and click!

TACTIC #10:

The "Do nothing e-mail"

This tactic (like most in this guide), refers to those list owners with low click-rates…

So, if you had enough with these low open or/and click through rates just try to send a series of e-mails that contains nothing but useful information about your niche/industry.

Of course, you understand that you must prepare the series of e-mails beforehand. Add as much value as possible.

REMEMBER: NO ACTIONT CALLS. The only promotion I recommend to these series of e-mails is to add your promotional link/URL at the end of the e-mail subject as a "PS:"

This is a great way to provide free value and change the way many of your hesitant subscribers see you or your business.

Also, whenever I do this "free educational e-mail series" I have noticed increased click-through rates as the series progresses.

People love free stuff from you (especially good advice) if they are interested in your stuff (I suppose they are... since they signed up in your list). If the free stuff is a discreet (or not) sales-funnel to your actual offer, then you might see a huge increase in clicks and sales.-

I recommend you apply the "Do-nothing" e-mail series frequently and of course... **Test tEst teSt tesT!**

TACTIC #11:

The magical URL (HIGHLY VALUED STRATEGY)

In order to use this strategy you might need certain script or software or just a code tweak, BUT it really works wonders and it increases the click through rate of your e-mail campaigns to unimaginable levels! Seriously.-

The idea is to present a link inside your e-mail body (maybe do a series of e-mails for this) that you will mention it is a "magical link"! If you click this link 3 times you will get 3 different bonuses. If you click the link 10 times you will get 10 different bonuses. If you click the link 100 times you will get 100 bonuses etc.

So, first you must have the backend that will redirect the user (who reads the e-mail and clicks the link) to a different URL every time he/she clicks the link ;)

Then you can set up as many offers, bonuses, articles, free info (endless possibilities) for these different URLs.

This is a great (and magical!) way to promote a lot of products (or sales funnels) via a single e-mail.

BUT you have to do it very appealing. You can introduce it as the "*magical link*" "*link of magic*" "magic fountain" etc.. Think of something that's related to your niche.

Can you see the potential of this?

Of course, I understand there's the difficult part to create the script that will redirect the user to the different URL's but even if you need to invest money for this, the results you will get, can make you a lot more money than what you invested. You can do this when you have the money.

TACTIC #12:

I have noticed (and it has been validated with many other list owners also) that if you want to have increased click-through rates (who doesn't?) you need to present appealing URLs for the user to click on.

For example if you are signed up with some affiliate network like Clickbank you get your unique promotional URL with which you promote a product. With most affiliate offers your unique affiliate URL will contain your affiliate username (another tip about that later).

But guess what? Internet users get more and more educated and some of them don't like affiliates or they might prefer to type the URL of the main domain without your affiliate reference just to have fun outsmarting an affiliate!

So, what you need to do is cloak your affiliate links so they appear 100% more appealing to the user who reads the e-mail. You can use a simple re-direct. This way you also protect your hard earned cash from affiliate-thieves.

The strategy depends on your niche. For example if you are on weight loss niche, then the URL's of your offers should include the keyword "weight loss" or similar words that will make the user curious about what's behind the link and click on it!

Of course you can use this tactic even if you are not an affiliate and you want to present more appealing URLs about your products/services.

A lot of tests have showed that when using targeted keywords in your URLs, you get increased click-through rates.

IF YOU DON'T KNOW HOW TO CLOAK/MASK YOUR AFFILIATE URL'S OR OTHER URL'S CHECK THIS FROM ME:
http://fiverr.com/nextnet/show-you-untold-secrets-to-get-your-emails-opened-and-your-links-clicked

TACTIC #13:

This tactic refers to affiliate offers. So, if you're promoting affiliate offers to your subscribers you can use it to see your click-through rates sky-rocketing!

The idea is to think before you sign up to an affiliate network. Be very careful about the username that you select. For example if you choose the username "johnmarketing" there is a great chance that your affiliate URL includes your username.

This makes a lot of people (as mentioned in previous tip) stripe the part of the URL with your affiliate username and they go and buy the product without generating the commission for you. Sad but true, sometimes.

So, to override this reaction, you can create an account with the affiliate network entering/choosing a "SMART" username like:

freebonus
claimbonus
freeversion

etc. so your affiliate URL contains one of the above words or similar. It is highly unlikely for a user to be tempted to delete the word "freebonus" from a URL.

This is a great way to protect your commissions and also... increase click-through rate, which is the main goal of this guide!

If you don't want to bother opening another account with an affiliate network, you can always mask your URLs as discussed in previous tactic.

TACTIC 14:

Improve your CALL TO ACTION

I've seen a lot of list owners missing this important information and I bet they have really low click-through rates...

They do not have a strong "Call To Action" in their e-mail messages.

The whole idea is to tell the user that you want him/her click the link! Many webmasters do not even use the "click here" phrase.

Always include that!

But you can use even stronger phrases and words to get the user make the desired click.

Again, this can be niche-specific but here's an example of what I mean:

"What I want you to do right now is move your mouse over the link below, click on it, and go download this free guide:"

I am sure you get my point.

Tell the users exactly what you want them to do.

TACTIC #15:

This tactic is similar to the one about taking advantage of the power of your "Thank You" pages...

The "Thank You" page is a static page where the user usually has no options but to close the window/tab.

The idea is to add an "Exit Pop-up" script to your "Thank You" page so whenever the subscriber closes the window/tab they are redirected to an one-time-offer or they are presented with another free download which might be a sales funnel for another one of your products or an affiliate offer.

Again, possibilities are endless with this strategy.

Just take advantage of your "Thank You" pages and you will see your overall earnings increased.

If you have more than one products then you can promote product/service A in the "Exit Pop-up" of the "Thank You" page that collects subscribers for product/service B and so on...

Please understand this strategy. It is powerful, especially if you have many offers/products/services to promote (even better if you can find affiliate offers to promote).

Also a great way to introduce users to more of you or more of your business.

Anything to re-capture the traffic!

TACTIC #16:

The magical archive (SUPER COOL!)

This one is used by very little people. In fact I've met just a couple of mailing list owners only, who do this.

It can be used when you are giving download links to your subscribers to get a free pdf report, a bonus etc.

The idea is to provide a zipped file instead of the actual pdf or other file.

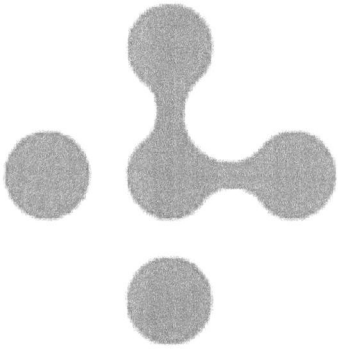

Inside the archive put the actual pdf and a second pdf file named "Super Cool Bonuses" for example.

In this second pdf file, start with a heading like "*Try this amazing new products/offers/services*" or "*Please find out more about my other products by clicking below*"…

Then add clickable links to your other offers/products/services (or affiliate offers)…

So the user who will read your e-mail, click the link and download the zipped file, will see a second pdf file (or even text file) called "Super Cool Bonuses". Chances are they will open it and hopefully they will be intrigued by the bonuses and offers in there and click the links.

That's more sales, more traffic and it can only help your site/business.

You can also apply this strategy with every product download you deliver ;)

TACTIC #17:

Increase social activity with bonuses (SUPER COOL)

This one is also… great. Just great! Put it to action and you can be amazed.

The idea is to use "Viral marketing" and let's say you offer a free pdf report to increase your subscribers base. You can create two or three reports (or maybe more). Maybe you can split a single report into more parts.

Then in your e-mail, offer the first part for free and mention that if they want the second part they should like you on facebook, then to get the third part they should follow you on twitter or youtube.

To expand your reach you can ask users to recommend 3 or more of their friends to "Like" your facebook page and they will get the last and most important part of the report.

Again, the difficult part here is to "design" the right backend system that will verify the "Likes" and the invites etc. so you can deliver on your promises…

But apart from that (which can be outsourced), this idea is so brilliant and the the potential for increased viral awareness is huuuge...

There are autoresponder services (Like GetResponse for example) that add social tools at the footer of your e-mail messages. But this is a little different.

TACTIC #18:

Ask people to add you to their contacts. (TOP)

This is super important and it ensures deliverability of your e-mail messages.

Ask the user to "White-list" the e-mail address you are sending your messages from.

You can do that in the "Thank You" page and in the footer of every one of your e-mails. You can ask gently or tell people they might miss bonuses if they skip white-listing your e-mail address.

You can also say something like:

"I really don't want you to miss my next e-mail so please add my e-mail address to your contacts (white-list)"

Or...

"To get my next super-powerful download for free, be sure to add me to your contacts (white-list the following e-mail address...)

It's up to you and the type of people you gather in your list.

But don't forget to make this small request (white-listing) in every occasion. And don't forget to clearly tell the user which e-mail address to white-list!

Don't overdo it though. And remember, the user is more "hot" right after he/she signs up on your list.

TACTIC #19:

This tactic is about motivating your subscribers more and more. If you offer a download or a product/service then give it a discount and a deadline. Before you create the deadline, send an e-mail to your list letting them know that because they are on your list they learn about the discount first. Before anybody else.

Then keep e-mailing them, mentioning the deadline and what has happened since you started the discounted offer. If you already had success, tell people about it. Even better, ask from your converted users to send you some feedback or a mini-review to send to your list.

Another way to create anticipation is to let your subscribers know that you will soon offer your products/services or a new product/service with a discount for a limited time only.

Keep e-mailing them about the offer often, then one day prior the launch and of course while the offer is active.

A way to "hack" this tactic is to create a landing page saying that the offer has expired. Then e-mail your list saying that you have an offer for the next few hours of days depending on the number of users who will subscribe. Then direct them to the "Expired Offer" page.

So, when a user sees your e-mail and the offer and clicks on the link, he/she will be taken to the expired offer! They will think that seats are filled! This will create great anticipation.

In the "Expired" page you will say boldly that the doors will open up again soon (maybe add an opt-in form for early bird access!). Then a few days later send a message saying that you accept new members again and send them to the correct page ;)

TACTIC #20:

Resend the message to those who didn't open

To apply this tactic you need specific script or software. This could be part of your mailing list software or your mailing list or autoresponder provider.

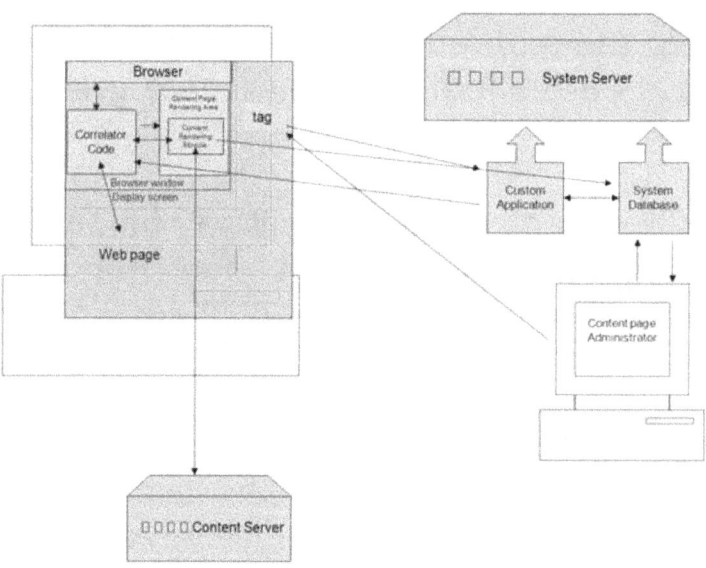

The idea is to group those users who didn't open your e-mail and send them and only them a second or third e-mail notice.

Believe me, this has worked wonders for many marketers and it is also used by many of them.

In your second e-mail a couple days later (or more) you can say something like:

"Hi, my staff reported that you didn't saw my last e-mail so... "

You can start with something like that and this will give a very personal tone to your message. When I tested, it produced really great results as I got clicks from people who didn't opened my first e-mail.

If I hadn't used this tactic, I doubt I would ever get those clicks (and sales) ;)

You can create curiosity with your subject line or with the e-mail body or both.

Be careful not to go too extreme with curiosity though. For example here's a subject line that's overboard:

"Hey. I saw your friend in the hospital today..."

;)

TACTIC #21:

Use curiosity to increase clicks

As mentioned, curiosity works wonders in e-mail marketing (and all forms of marketing).

You can create curiosity in your e-mails so as to get the desired click from the user and bring him/her in your website/landing page/offer/e-shop etc.

For example if you have a free download (sales funnel for one of your products or affiliate offers etc.) you might not reveal exactly what is included but you can say something like…:

"…this free pdf guide is delivered exclusively to the members of my list (that's you friend). Inside I reveal secret information that I am not supposed to tell anyone about. I am now sharing the rare info with people who will download and read the whole pdf report…"

Curiosity along with (anticipation) can bring wonderful results (increased click through rate).

TACTIC #22:

This tactic can be used in the same manner as the tactic with the "Thank You" page.

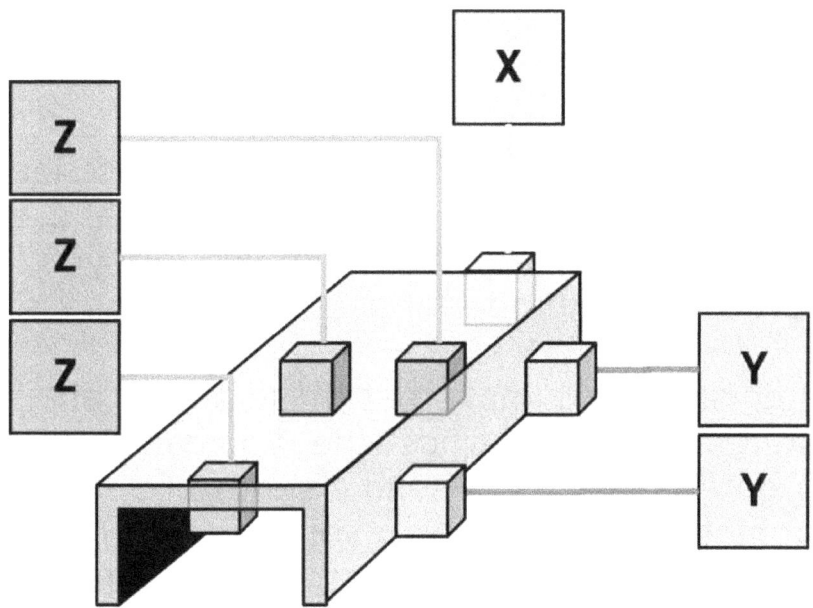

No matter what you do with your list and subscribers, there will always be people who will want to unsubscribe for any reason. Maybe they stopped enjoying your emails, maybe they are moving to a new territory and they want to stop receiving e-mails for a while. Maybe they lost access to their e-mail address or changed it. It doesn't matter.

First of all, you must have users truly unsubscribe if they wish to. Do not use a fake unsubscribe system. I've seen many marketers using fake unsubscribe systems and when people are unsubscribed from one list they are automatically subscribed to a dozen of other lists and they are bombarded with e-mails. This is pure spam and totally unethical right?

But what you can do is keep the unsubscribed e-mails to a separate list for later ethical use and don't send e-mails to that list until you have a large number of users gathered.

Then since you know that these people are interested in a specific niche, you can make targeted mailings or send a series of promotional e-mails with your offers. Of course you will offer them the option to unsubscribe again.

You can send this list e-mails from a different address so they will not know it came from a list they have already unsubscribed.

You can also add links or banners to your unsubscribe page to direct users to other products/services, affiliate offers etc.

Again, use your imagination, possibilities are endless!

TACTIC #23:

Blog your e-mail messages (BRILLIANT!)

This tactic is never used by most marketers but it is so smart and easy to do (copy and paste).

Instead of just writing a compelling e-mail and sending it to your list you can also post that e-mail message to your blog or website.

Think about it. When you write an e-mail message you put all your efforts to write compelling content for readers to find useful and click on your links.

Why not put this piece of promotional text in your blog too?

I believe it is a great idea.

I don't mean you should do it with every e-mail you are preparing for your list, but I am sure there are times you write more inspired content than other times.

So, you should know when an e-mail message would be helpful for your blog visitors/readers too. If you feel like it, go ahead and post it there. You got nothing to lose and a lot to gain...!

CLOSING

SO THAT WAS ALL!

The most important thing in e-mail marketing according to my opinion is "Split testing".

I'm sure you've heard marketers telling you that you should test, test and then again go and make some tests…

And this is true.

Unless you make tests and calibrate your e-mail campaigns to fit your list and your niche/industry perfectly, it is hard to achieve high goals (more money)…

So go ahead, read this guide one more time (or even more), apply the tactics, adjust them to your needs or niche/industry and measure the results.

I am confident that if you use the tactics in a smart and consistent way, you will see tremendous results.

Good luck!

Apply what you've learned, make tests, experiments, have consistency in your actions and overall behavior, and I believe you will create wonders.

I wish you success and happiness beyond any extend!

If you find the time, leave me a positive review for this book on Amazon (this is deeply appreciated and if you message me I will send you another one of my books for free), check some of my books here:
http://amazon.com/author/lazarosgeorgoulas/

CREDITS

First I would like to thank my co-worker, editor and a person I really appreciate, Maria Markella. I love you. Thank you for your on-going support.

All images from Wikimedia Commons: http://commons.wikimedia.org

Image credits:

MG - http://commons.wikimedia.org/wiki/File:AROBAZE.png

Mikrop88 - http://commons.wikimedia.org/wiki/File:3-2-1_Regel_Flaechenprinzip.png

Pvdkerk - http://commons.wikimedia.org/wiki/File:Affiliate_marketing.jpg

AromaWebDesign - http://commons.wikimedia.org/wiki/File:Aroma_web_design.jpg

Diego Interlaced - http://commons.wikimedia.org/wiki/File:Cloud_Communication.jpg

Alan J. Edwards - http://commons.wikimedia.org/wiki/File:Content_Rendering_Control_System_and_Method_Figure.jpg

Megapixie - http://commons.wikimedia.org/wiki/File:Disruptivetechnology.gif

Felippewilkinson - http://commons.wikimedia.org/wiki/File:Felippe_Wilkinson.jpg

Finally, I want to thank all my readers and especially those who saw the potential of the tactics in this book and found the time to go and leave a positive review on Amazon!

www.ingramcontent.com/pod-product-compliance
Lightning Source LLC
Chambersburg PA
CBHW071817170526
45167CB00003B/1339